W9-AJT-007

Bloomfield Twp. Public Library
1099 Lone Pine Road
Bloomfield Hills, MI 48302-2410

WORLD OF SPORTS

SKATEBOARDING

Published by Smart Apple Media
1980 Lookout Drive, North Mankato, Minnesota 56003

Copyright © 2003 Smart Apple Media. International
copyright reserved in all countries. No part of this book
may be reproduced in any form without written per-
mission from the publisher.

Photographs by AllSport (Mike Powell), Ron Church,
Icon Sports Media (Tony Donaldson), David Madison
Sports Images, SportsChrome (Rob Tringali Jr.,
Michael Zito)

Design and production by EvansDay Design

LIBRARY OF CONGRESS CATALOGING-IN-PUBLICATION DATA

McAuliffe, Bill.
Skateboarding / by Bill McAuliffe.
p. cm. — (World of sports)
Includes Index.
Summary: Describes the history, equipment, and
techniques of skateboarding.
ISBN 1-58340-162-8
1. Skateboarding—Juvenile literature. [1. Skateboarding.]
I. Title. II. World of sports (North Mankato, Minn.).

GV859.8 .M394 2002
796.22—dc21   2001049929

First Edition
9 8 7 6 5 4 3 2 1

SKATE BOARDING

BILL McAULIFFE

Bloomfield Twp. Public Library
1099 Lone Pine Road
Bloomfield Hills, MI 48302-2410

Skateboarding is being scared
and doing it anyway. It's
hanging on and making it. It's
hangin' and slamming.... For
the man, skateboarding is free-
dom and youth rediscovered; for
the boy, a means of self-expres-
sion vital to his being. For you
see, skateboarding is the blood,
rolling through his veins.

Dave Hackett, PROFESSIONAL
SKATEBOARDER

MAY 2 0 2003

Grabbing Air, Scraping Skin

━━━

During the day, the streets downtown are filled with the sounds of hammering, horns, sirens, and crowds. At night, a different sound emerges. That's when the sound of wood clattering against pavement echoes among the tall buildings as skateboarders take their new tricks to the center of town. Pavement is what a skateboarder needs, and downtown has plenty of it. Curbs, benches, rails, planters, driveways, and stairways all add to the challenge.

Vernon Courtland Johnson designed the first skull image for a skateboard in the late 1970s. It resembled the cover of a musical album by the band Emerson, Lake, and Palmer.

Across town, dozens of skateboarders hurl themselves up ramps, along ledges, and around the curved bowls at the local skatepark. A few parents sit nearby, watching or reading, paying no attention to the hip-hop music blasting over the loudspeakers.

Although the average age of a **skater** is about 14, skateboarding is fast becoming one of the top five participant sports in the United States. The *Wall Street Journal* reported that participation more than doubled from 1992 to 2000. Since the X Games first brought "extreme" sports to a

wide television audience in 1995, skateboard sales have tripled to $72 million annually. And as a result, skatepark construction has increased dramatically.

Skaters say the reasons for the sport's popularity are obvious. It's fun. It's risky. It looks cool. It's on television and in the movies. Simply put, there's nothing like the basic thrill of taking off on your skateboard—getting **big air**, twisting or sliding along a ledge, or balancing on the board out in space.

Adding to skateboarding's appeal is the fact that there are no boundaries, teams, uniforms, coaches, or scores. "There are some contests, but they're not indicative of who's best," said the manager of one skatepark in Minneapolis, Minnesota. "Nobody's ever *won* at skateboarding. It's a sport, but it's more of an art form. If you can make that trick that you're working on today, that's what counts."

An independent spirit is a big part of skateboarding. Skaters of-

Skateboarding was declared a "hazardous activity" in 1997. This means that skaters cannot blame cities if they hurt themselves on public property. As a result, cities now worry less about potential lawsuits from injured skaters.

skater   *a skateboarder*

big air   *great height or distance when jumping*

THE PUNK ROCK CLOTH-
ING AND ATTITUDES OF
MANY SKATEBOARDERS
HAVE GIVEN THE SPORT A
REBELLIOUS REPUTATION.

street *skateboarding on side-walks, benches, steps, rails, or other structures found in public places*

rebellious *opposed to what is commonly accepted*

banned *made illegal*

ten think they are the only ones who understand the sport. As a group, they often dress similarly. In the 1960s, "sidewalk surfers" skated barefoot in bell-bottom pants. By 2000, the typical outfit included specially designed skateboard shoes, low-hanging, baggy pants, big shirts, and beanie stocking caps or baseball caps worn backwards. Skaters gravitate toward the aggressive rhythms of hip-hop, rap, or heavy metal music, incorporating the beats into their skating moves. Reggae is also a favorite.

Street skaters often have a youthful, **rebellious** attitude. That may be a learned attitude. After all, skaters can't be afraid to fall hard on concrete. But some say it's been forced on them. Many cities and smaller business districts have **banned** public skateboarding. Officials say it's dangerous to pedestrians and destroys property. Police in many cities can give skaters tickets or **confiscate** their boards. Even so, many street skaters are determined to skate wherever they find a challenging structure or piece of pavement. "Skateboarding is not a crime," they say. But they often are chased away by building owners or police.

Skateboard magazines and graphics often portray skaters as dark, angry, and hostile toward society. Images of skulls began appearing on skateboards in the late 1970s, and a successful Canadian skateboard manufacturer called itself Skull Skates. Today, phrases such as "Skate or Die" or "Skate and Destroy" are popular.

Skateboard magazines emphasize the creative physical skills of top skaters. They try to sell skateboard products with sophisticated advertising and photography. But they also tend to make light of alcohol abuse and other destructive behaviors. For this reason, some stores have refused to

In the 1960s, when surfing helped create skateboarding, skateboarders often skated as they might surf—barefoot. As tricks became popular, though, it became more and more important to wear shoes while skating.

sell particular skateboarding magazines. Home-published skateboard **zines** mix skateboard news, interviews, and music reviews with material geared toward adult readers.

Despite all of this, skateboarding is gaining popularity within the **mainstream**. A skateboard demonstration at a fair, shopping center, or major sporting event attracts people of all ages, who applaud the skaters' skill and admire their breathtaking tricks.

confiscate *to take away a person's possession through legal means*

zines *magazines that are published cheaply, often on home computers, for small audiences that share a common interest*

mainstream *the greatest number of like-minded people in a society; "normal," not "extreme"*

SKATEPARKS OFFER SKATERS OF ALL ABILITY LEVELS THE SPACE AND EQUIPMENT TO EXPAND THEIR SKILLS.

Many parents have come to believe that skating is okay for their kids. Many are happy to take their kids to skateparks. There, helmets are required, lessons are given, the skating surfaces are smoother than concrete, and all activity is supervised. Skateparks have grown in number and today are even popular places for birthday parties.

Frank Nasworthy's urethane wheels were called "Cadillac Wheels" because they made skateboarders feel as though they were gliding in a luxurious Cadillac car.

One mother at a Minneapolis skatepark said she thought skateboarding appealed to her son because he could develop leg strength and coordination. Even though she was worried her son might get injured, she said skateboarding was one thing that would get him away from computer games. "He's out here being athletic instead of at home with a video game," she said. "It's a lot better."

An Up-and-Down History

■ ━━━━━ ■

Skateboarding was invented hundreds of times over the years. Basically, every time a kid lost a roller skate and nailed a board to the remaining skate, he or she created a skateboard.

In the 1960s, when **surfing** became popular, some manufacturers, such as Makaha, found ways that kids who didn't live near the ocean could pretend to surf. They began making boards with wheels attached to the bottom. These "sidewalk surfers" were flat and usually had steel or clay wheels that were noisy and slippery. The boards were also hard to maneuver.

Most skateboarders say the sport is difficult to learn and requires countless hours of practice. Skaters fall a lot and can get hurt. But most skateparks offer lessons to people of all skill levels.

Still, California skateboarders discovered they could do some exciting moves by skating around the slopes, up the walls, and along the **coping** of empty swimming pools. Soon skateboards became so popular that international contests were held, and skateboarding was featured in movies and magazines. In 1964, one of the biggest American musical

groups at the time, Jan and Dean, had a hit song called "Sidewalk Surfin'." A short film called "Skater Dater" won an Academy Award in 1965.

But soon after this burst of skateboard fever, the California Medical Association stated that skateboarding was causing more injuries to children than bicycling. In 1965, *Life* magazine had a cover story on "the craze and the menace of skateboarding." That same year, cities began to enforce skateboarding bans, and skateboards seemed to vanish.

In 1971, however, a California surfer built a skateboard with the back tipped up. Leaning on this "kicktail," skateboarders could do quick, sharp turns and stay in control. In 1973, another surfer named Frank Nasworthy discovered that a new type of roller skate wheel was even more effective on skateboards. Made of a plastic called urethane, the wheels were quiet and gripped well. Soon after, a

Modern skateparks feature ramps and pools made from a smooth material called Skatelite. When skaters fall in these parks, they slide down without getting scraped.

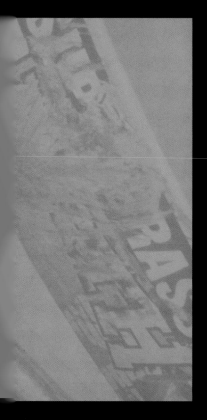

surfing *riding a board on waves on the ocean*

coping *the rim (often metal or tile) at the top of an incline or around the edge of a swimming pool*

flexible *able to bend*

hardcore *intensely dedicated or extreme*

vert *vertical; skating that usually involves a ramp*

WIDELY REGARDED AS A HAZARDOUS ACTIVITY IN ITS EARLY YEARS, SKATE-BOARDING HAS GROWN BY LEAPS AND BOUNDS.

surfboard manufacturer named Bob Bahne started making **flexible** skateboards out of fiberglass. The plastic material helped skateboarders shift their weight more effectively. Now they could do wilder tricks than before. Pool skaters even discovered they could push off walls into the air!

In 1975, skateboard contests became popular again in California. The next year, the first modern skateboard parks were built in Daytona, Florida, and Carlsbad, California. Skateboarding also became popular in Europe. In the late 1970s, a young Florida skater named Alan "Ollie" Gelfand figured out a way to pop his skateboard into the air off of a flat surface. Soon, "getting air" became the goal of nearly all skaters.

A short time later, BMX biking hit the scene. Skateboarders began to move toward more aggressive styles and adopt punk and new wave music. Again, they were viewed as troublemakers. Skateboard parks began to close, and the sport seemed to fade away again.

But skateboarders didn't disappear. As BMX biking became popular, many **hardcore** skaters felt left out. But they rallied when *Thrasher* magazine debuted in 1981. The magazine was written by and for skateboarders. Slowly, the sport began to flourish, again with an emphasis on **vert** riding as well as streetstyle. Some of the most famous skaters in the sport's history began to emerge, including Tony Hawk and Steve Caballero.

Hawk was part of a professional skating team called the Bones Brigade. The team skated for an equipment manufacturer, Powell Peralta. It toured Europe and made exciting videos that introduced new skating moves and styles. Today, Hawk is one of the best-known skaters in the world and has helped create several top-selling video games. He even owns a skateboard company.

In-line skating, also known as rollerblading, cut into skateboarding's popularity in the early 1990s. But skateboarding didn't fade away. Many parents who had skateboarded in the 1960s and '70s now had children who were interested in the sport. In 1995, when the ESPN television network included skateboarding in its international X Games, interest in the sport exploded again. Downhill skateboarding regained its popularity as street luge. Street luge riders navigate large skateboards down steep, narrow

RIDERS OF STREET LUGE, THE NEXT GENERATION OF DOWNHILL SKATE-BOARDING, TRAVEL AT GREAT SPEEDS.

TONY HAWK HAS BE-
COME THE WORLD'S
MOST FAMOUS SKATE-
BOARDER, THANKS
LARGELY TO HIS MANY
ENDORSEMENTS.

streets while lying on their backs.

Today, skateboard shoes, clothing, and other equipment are sold to lots of people who aren't even skateboarders. Professional skaters, who

Some skatepark builders incorporate portable ramps, rails, and other structures that can be moved around for events and demonstrations. Such changes also add to the fun and challenge of the parks.

let companies use their names on shoes or boards, can make incredible sums of money through competitions and endorsements. Some skaters believe money, advertising, and show business have affected the sport too much. They think the sport has lost its rebellious spirit. Others believe its huge popularity will keep it strong.

Decks, Trucks, and Wheels

Most modern skateboards are made of many layers of wood pressed into a single solid piece. They are angled up at both ends to make it easy to tip the board to do tricks. A standard **deck** is about 33 inches (84 cm) long and 7 to 10 inches (18–25 cm) wide at its widest point. The tops are generally covered with a gritty, black, sandpapery material that keeps skaters' feet from slipping. Some skaters apply sticky tape to help them grip the board.

Early skateparks had snake-like concrete courses. Modern skateparks now include some street features, such as rails and ledges. But street skaters prefer actual streets and sidewalks.

The top of a board has to have traction. But stylish bottoms, with their artistic designs, bold labels, and stickers, make skateboards look like racecars. They're decorated that way partly because most pictures of skaters doing tricks show the bottom of the skateboard.

Skaters sometimes attach small, plastic rails to the bottoms of their skateboards to help them grab the edges when they're in the air. These also help the board slide smoothly on rails and ledges.

The **trucks** are the devices that connect the wheels to the deck. They include rubber inserts that help the skateboards absorb shocks and turn. Trucks can be adjusted for different styles of skating and different size skaters. Wheels also come in different sizes and can be hard or soft. Beginners do better on softer wheels. Wheels also have varying **diameters**. Smaller wheels go faster, but they also wear out quicker.

A deck, truck, and wheels costs about $100, or less at a

Skateboarder, the sport's original magazine, was published from 1975 until 1982. Thrasher was launched in 1981 and is still one of the most popular skateboard magazines published today.

deck *the skateboard itself; the wooden platform*

trucks *metal arms attached to the bottom of a skateboard that hold the wheels and cushioning*

diameters *the distance from one edge of a wheel to the other, through the middle; the width*

EVEN THE MOST EXPERIENCED SKATERS RECOGNIZE THE NEED FOR HEAD, ELBOW, AND KNEE PROTECTION.

used sporting goods store. But skate-boarders also should have elbow and kneepads, a helmet, and gloves. Elbow and kneepads are usually *Transworld Skateboard-ing, another popular skateboard magazine, is published by the same company that publishes* Field and Stream *and* Popular Science. covered with plastic plates for added protection. Kneepads are very bulky, which is another reason skateboarders wear baggy pants. This protective equipment can cost up to an-other $100.

PROTECTIVE EQUIP-MENT IS ESPECIALLY IMPORTANT FOR VERT SKATERS, WHO MAY TAKE SPILLS AT AWK-WARD ANGLES.

SKATEBOARD SHOES ARE DESIGNED TO MAINTAIN CLOSE CONTACT WITH A DECK'S ROUGH SURFACE.

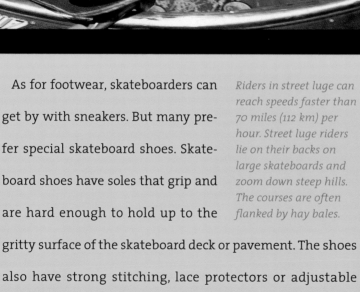

As for footwear, skateboarders can get by with sneakers. But many prefer special skateboard shoes. Skateboard shoes have soles that grip and are hard enough to hold up to the gritty surface of the skateboard deck or pavement. The shoes also have strong stitching, lace protectors or adjustable straps, and extra heel padding to prevent bruises.

Riders in street luge can reach speeds faster than 70 miles (112 km) per hour. Street luge riders lie on their backs on large skateboards and zoom down steep hills. The courses are often flanked by hay bales.

sequences *groups of action photos taken several seconds apart, usually with a motor-driven camera*

SKATEBOARDS ARE BUILT TO LOOK GOOD AND TO WITH-STAND THE PUNISHMENT OF JUMPS AND TRICKS.

Skateboard shoes offer a lot of protection around the toes. That's because the toes are often used to balance, flip, or spin the board. Skateboard shoes cost $80 or more. They're widely popular and sold in all kinds of shoe stores—not just skateboard shops. Many are named for professional skaters.

At the 1999 X Games, at the age of 31, famed skater Tony Hawk performed the world's first two-and-a-half twist skateboard jump on his 12th try. He then retired, though he continued to make occasional appearances.

There's one other important piece of skateboarding equipment: a camera. Many skaters like to record their tricks either on video or in **sequences**.

A Board and Body

■━━━━━━■

For many skaters, skateboarding is all about the tricks. Some tricks borrow their names from surfing, drag racing, or other sports. But in skateboard magazines, videos, and demonstrations, on the street and in the skatepark, there are a lot of unusual words used to describe what the skaters are doing. The language changes as fast as the position of a skater's feet, so a person needs to pay close attention!

At the 2001 Nickelodeon Kids' Choice Awards, Tony Hawk was voted Favorite Male Sports Star. Nickelodeon is a cable television channel that specializes in off-beat kids' programming and syndicated sitcoms from the past 40 years.

Some terms describe how skaters stand on the board. "Regular" skaters always start with their left foot forward. Skaters who lead with their right foot are said to skate "goofy." If they spend a few minutes skating the other way, they are skating **switch**. But when they skate tail (back) first, that's **fakie**.

One of the most basic skateboard moves is called the "pump." To pump, skaters ride up an incline and back down without turning the board. They bend and straighten their legs to gain speed. A "tick-tock," meanwhile, is a turning move in which skaters lift the front of

the board and move it from side to side to turn, instead of lean-

ing. A third basic move is called a "manual." In a manual,

skaters roll with either the front or back wheels in the air.

World-famous skate-boarder Tony Hawk skates "goofy," which means he skates with his right foot first. Most skaters skate with their left foot forward.

    In a trick known as an "ollie," skaters press down on the tail

of the board to lift the board's nose (front), move their lead foot back slightly toward

the middle, then jump. All the while, the skaters keep their feet in contact with the

board—without grabbing it. An ollie enables skaters to jump over some things and

onto others. The most basic skateboard jump, the ollie is the trick upon which almost

all other skateboard tricks are based. A "nollie" is an ollie that leads with the tail.

    Some tricks require skaters to momentarily separate themselves from their board.

In a "pop shove-it," skaters jump into the air while spinning the board so that the tail

end moves to the front. They then land back on the board. Skaters usually practice

this on grass or carpet to minimize injury.

switch *with the opposite foot forward*

fakie *in the opposite direction, usually backwards or tail-first*

MANY SKATERS TODAY EN-
JOY THE CHALLENGE AND
RISKS OF RIDING THEIR
BOARDS DOWN HANDRAILS.

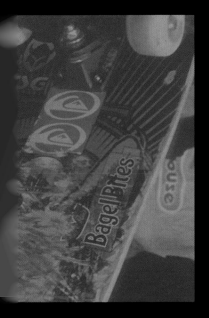

BASIC MOVES SUCH AS
THE PUMP AND THE
TICK-TOCK MUST BE MAS-
TERED BEFORE RIDERS
CAN ATTEMPT GRABS.

One of the most popular maneu-
vers today is a "boardslide." As the
name suggests, this is a straight-
ahead slide down a rail or along a
ledge. The slide is on the bottom of
the board instead of the wheels. The board has to be crosswise to the rail or ledge to accomplish this. Skaters who ro-
tate the board a quarter turn from a boardslide might find
themselves doing "grinds," sliding along the rail or ledge on
the board's trucks.

Riding down handrails caught on in the early 1990s. Today,
boardslides, grinds, and similar tricks are the most commonly photographed skateboard moves. But there are
dozens of other specific moves and variations, often used in
combination with one another. A "bluntslide," for example,

In 1976, skater Jack Smith and two friends skateboarded from Lebanon, Oregon, to Williamsburg, Virginia, in 32 days. Smith crossed the United States again in 1984, this time in just 26 days.

27

is a boardslide with one end of the board tipped up. A "lip-slide" is a ride crosswise on the front edge of the board along a rail or ledge. The rest of the board is out to the side.

Balancing positions are dramatic ways to start routines or stop action midway through a sequence. One particularly difficult move requires skaters to balance one wheel on top of a rail or ledge, leaving the other three suspended in space. A "five-oh" is a grind with the front truck in the air—an impressive beginning balance trick. Some skaters reverse this move and ride with the front truck on a rail or ledge and the back in the air.

The first skateboards were very narrow. Canadian Willi Winkel developed the first wide skateboards in the 1970s. One of his early creations had eight wheels.

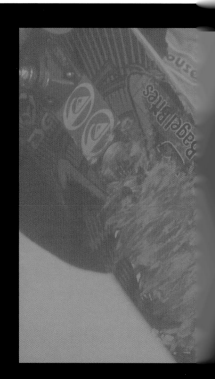

"Grabs" are a family of moves in which skaters grab the board with a hand while in the air. They grab the board between their feet with either their trailing or lead hand, depending upon the trick. A "stale fish" is a jump off a ramp in which skaters grab the backside of the board with their trailing hand while turning.

SKATEBOARDING HAS SURGED IN POPULARITY, DUE LARGELY TO SUCH TELEVISED COMPETITIONS AS THE X GAMES.

AS MORE YOUNG PEOPLE TAKE
UP THE SPORT, THE SKY IS THE
LIMIT FOR SKATEBOARDING
IN ALL ITS FORMS.

"Kickflips" were invented by skater Rodney Mullen in 1983. He called them "magic flips." A kickflip begins with the toes. It involves spinning the board wheels-over-deck underneath the skater's feet during a jump. More advanced skaters may attempt to flip the board with their heels instead of their toes.

The 1985 hit movie Back to the Future, starring Michael J. Fox, featured a futuristic skateboard called a hoverboard, which rode on air.

Steve Caballero invented the "cab full-revolution jump," in which skaters lead with their board's tail, standing with the opposite foot in the lead. The move can also be performed with only half a twist. Like most skateboarding tricks, this trick requires a lot of practice. And some tricks, no matter how effortless they may look, should only be attempted with instruction from a professional—and plenty of protective equipment.

The Continuing Saga

In 1976, three young men skateboarded across the United States. The sport of skateboarding seemed to follow. Today, skateboarding is no longer just a pastime for out-of-the-water surfers in California. It is popular in small towns and cities all over the world. In fact, skaters from Philadelphia, Pennsylvania, dominated at the 2001 X Games.

The highest "ollie" (a skateboarding jump maneuver) performed from flat ground measured 44 ½ inches (113 cm). Skater Danny Wainwright made the record jump.

John Street, the mayor of Philadelphia, host city to the 2001 X Games, is a skateboarding fan. His 13-year-old son is an avid skater. Street said he knows that many parents think skateboarding is dangerous for their kids. He thinks parents need to understand that their kids have a different view of sports.

"I tell them [other parents], 'Welcome to a whole new century,'" Street said. "It's just part of the change that's going on in the world of athletics, and the sooner people get adjusted to it, the better."